USING THIS BOOK

*One of the best ways of helping children to learn to read is by reading stories to them and with them. This way they learn what **reading** is, and they will gradually come to recognise many words, and begin to read for themselves.*

First, grown-ups read the story on the left-hand pages aloud to the child.

You can reread the story as often as the child enjoys hearing it. Talk about the pictures as you go.

Later the child will read the words under the pictures on the right-hand page.

The pages at the back of the book will give you some ideas for helping your child to read.

British Library Cataloguing in Publication Data

McCullagh, Sheila K.
    Tim Catchamouse. — (Puddle Lane. Series no. 855. Stage 1; v. 1)
    1. Readers — 1950-
    I. Title   II. Morris, Tony, *1938 Aug 2-*   III. Series
    428.6   PE1119
    ISBN 0-7214-0909-1

First edition

Published by Ladybird Books Ltd Loughborough Leicestershire UK
Ladybird Books Inc Lewiston Maine 04240 USA

© Text and presentation SHEILA McCULLAGH MCMLXXXV
© In publication LADYBIRD BOOKS LTD MCMLXXXV

Tim Catchamouse

written by SHEILA McCULLAGH
illustrated by TONY MORRIS

This book belongs to:

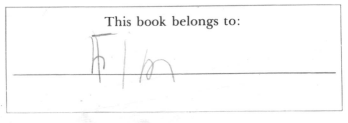

Ladybird Books

Timothy Catchamouse was
a little black cat.
'Timothy Catchamouse' was
a very long name for a very little cat,
so everyone called him 'Tim'.

Tim lived in a hole under the steps
of a very old house.
He lived there with his mother,
and his sister, Tessa.

Tim

His mother's name was Peggoty,
but everyone called her 'Pegs'.

Pegs

One day, Pegs was going out.
"You can play in the garden
while I'm away," she said.
"But remember this:
a magician lives in the house.
Everyone says that he's **very** grumpy.
So if you meet the Magician,
you must be **very** polite."

"I'll remember," said Tim.

Tim and Pegs

Pegs went out.
She ran across the garden
to the old iron gate.

She crept under the gate, and
out into the lane.

Pegs went out.

Tim looked at his sister.

She was fast asleep.

Tim jumped on her, to wake her up.

But she only said, "Go away!" and
went back to sleep again.

Tim jumped.

Tim looked out of the hole.
The sun was shining.
The sky was blue.

Tim went out, into the garden.

Tim went out.

Tim saw a tree.

The tree was growing near the house.

Tim saw a tree.

Tim ran to the tree,
and began to climb up it.

Tim ran to the tree.

Tim climbed to the very top
of the tree.

He looked down and saw the house.

The roof of the house
was very close
to the top of the tree.

Tim looked down.

Tim jumped on to the roof
of the house.

There was a window
in the roof.

Tim saw the window.
The window was open.

Tim saw the window.

Tim ran up the roof
to the window.

He looked down into
the room below.

He saw an old man
sitting in a chair.
The old man
had long white hair,
and a white beard.

"He must be the Magician,"
Tim said to himself.

the Magician

The Magician was fast asleep.

Tim leaned over,
to have a good look at him.
But his foot slipped —
and he fell in!

He landed right on the Magician's knee!

Tim dug in his claws, and held on.

Tim fell in.

The Magician woke up
with a yell of pain.
He saw Tim standing on his knee.

"Where on earth did you come from?"
he asked.

"I fell in," said Tim.

"Then you'd better fall out again,"
said the Magician.
"Take your claws out of my knee,
and go away!"

The Magician woke up.

Tim pulled out his claws.
He looked up at the window.

"I can't get up there
by myself," he said.

Tim looked up.

"We'll soon see about that,"
said the Magician.
"One, two, three —
and you're back in the tree!"
He snapped his fingers.

One, two, three —

Tim felt himself flying up in the air.
A moment later,
he found himself back
in the top of the tree.

— and Tim
was in the tree.

Tim climbed down the tree,
just as Pegs came back
into the garden.

Tim ran to meet her.

"Tim!" cried Pegs.
"Where **have** you been?"

Tim ran.

"I've been to see the Magician,"
said Tim. "It was very exciting."

"I expect it was," said Pegs.
"But you'd better be careful, Tim.
Magicians can work magic."

"I know they can," said Tim.
"The Magician **did** work magic.
I flew up into the tree.
It was **very** exciting.
But I shall be very careful,
next time."

Tim and Pegs

Notes for the parent/teacher

When you have read the story, go back to the beginning. Look at each picture and talk about it, pointing to the caption below, and reading it aloud yourself.

Run your finger along under the words as you read, so that the child learns that reading goes from left to right. (You needn't say this in so many words. Children learn many useful things about reading by just reading with you, and it is often better to let them learn by experience, rather than by explanation.) When you next go through the book, encourage the child to read the words and sentences under the illustrations.

Mrs Pitter-Patter dropped the tail with a yell. She made such a noise, that she woke Mr Gotobed, who was fast asleep in bed in the house at the end of the lane.

Mr Gotobed woke up.

Don't rush in with the word before she* has time to think, but don't leave her floundering for too long. Always encourage her to feel that she is reading successfully, praising her when she does well, and avoiding criticism.

Now turn back to the beginning, and print the child's name in the space on the title page, using ordinary, not capital letters. Let her watch you print it: this is another useful experience.

*Children enjoy hearing the same story many times. Read this one as often as the child likes hearing it. The more opportunities she has of looking at the illustrations and **reading** the captions with you, the more she will come to recognise the words. Don't worry if she **remembers** rather than **reads** the captions. This is a normal stage in learning.*

If you have a number of books, let her choose which story she would like to have again.

**Footnote:* In order to avoid the continual "he or she", "him or her", the child is referred to in this book as "she". However, the stories are equally appropriate to boys and girls.

Puddle Lane Reading Programme Stage 1

There are several books at this Stage about the same characters. All the books at each Stage are separate stories and are written at the same reading level.

The lists below show other titles available at Stages 1 and 2.

Stage 1

1 Tim Catchamouse

2 Tessa and the Magician

3 The magic box

4 Mrs Pitter-Patter and the Magician

from Mrs Pitter-Patter and the Magician

Children should read as many books as possible at Stage 1 before going on to Stage 2.
Here are some stories from the next Stage which include other people and characters who live in Puddle Lane:

Stage 2

1 When the magic stopped
2 Tessa in Puddle Lane
3 The little monster

from The little monster